W9-AUZ-353

The publisher gratefully acknowledges the Military Child Education Coalition for their expert review of this book and for their authorship of a Note to Caregivers.

To brave kids everywhere. —BK

Staff for This Book

Erica Green, *Project Editor*
Amanda Larsen, *Art Director and Designer*
Lori Epstein, *Senior Photo Editor*
Callie Broaddus, *Associate Designer*
Debbie Gibbons, *Director of Maps*
Matthew Chwastyk, *Map Research and Production*
Paige Towler, *Editorial Assistant*
Sanjida Rashid and Rachel Kenny, *Design Production Assistants*
Tammi Colleary-Loach, *Rights Clearance Manager*
Mari Robinson and Michael Cassady, *Rights Clearance Specialists*
Grace Hill, *Managing Editor*
Joan Gossett, *Senior Production Editor*
Lewis R. Bassford, *Production Manager*
Jennifer Hoff, *Manager, Production Services*
Susan Borke, *Legal and Business Affairs*

Library of Congress Cataloging-in-Publication Data

Kerley, Barbara.
  Brave like me / by Barbara Kerley. -- 1st edition.
    pages cm
    Audience: Ages 4-8.
  Includes bibliographical references.
  ISBN 978-1-4263-2360-7 (hardback) -- ISBN 978-1-4263-2361-4 (library binding)
 1. Children of military personnel--United States--Juvenile literature. 2. Families of military personnel--United States--Juvenile literature. 3. Separation (Psychology) in children--Juvenile literature. I. Title.
  U766.K46 2016
  355.1'20973--dc23

                              2015027844

Printed in Hong Kong
15/THK/1

Photo Credits
Cover, U.S. Air Force/Airman 1st Class Gustavo Castillo; back cover, Image Source/Alamy; case cover, Lightix/Shutterstock; 1, David McNew/Getty Images; 2-3, Sandy Huffaker/Getty Images; 5, U.S. Air Force/Staff Sgt. Chris Willis; 6-7, Alliance Images/Alamy; 8, U.S. Air Force/1st Lt. Stephanie Schonberger; 9, Ariel Skelley/Blend Images/Getty Images; 10, rubberball/Getty Images; 12, Tom Odulate/Cultura RF/Getty Images; 13, Jupiterimages/Photolibrary RM/Getty Images; 14, U.S. Navy/Mass Communication Specialist 2nd Class Kilho Park; 15, U.S. Navy/Mass Communication Specialist 1st Class Joshua Davies; 16-17, U.S. Navy/Petty Officer 2nd Class Ernesto Hernandez Fonte; 18, blue jean images/Getty Images; 19, Janice Richard/E+/Getty Images; 20, Gary John Norman/The Image Bank/Getty Images; 21, John Howard/Getty Images; 22-23, Cultura RM/Zak Kendal/Getty Images; 24-25, U.S. Air Force/Staff Sgt. Shane A. Cuomo; 26, Donald Iain Smith/Blend Images RM/Getty Images; 27, Terry Vine/Blend Images RM/Getty Images; 28-29, U.S. Air Force/Staff Sgt. Renae Saylock; 30, U.S. Air National Guard/Master Sgt. Mark C. Olsen; 31, U.S. Air Force/Tech. Sgt. Samuel King Jr.; 32 (A), U.S. Air Force/Airman 1st Class Gustavo Castillo; 32 (B), David McNew/Getty Images; 32 (C), Sandy Huffaker/Getty Images; 32 (D), U.S. Air Force/Staff Sgt. Chris Willis; 32 (E), Alliance Images/Alamy; 32 (F), U.S. Air Force/1st Lt. Stephanie Schonberger; 32 (G), Ariel Skelley/Blend Images/Getty Images; 32 (H), rubberball/Getty Images; 32 (I), Tom Odulate/Cultura RF/Getty Images; 32 (J), Jupiterimages/Photolibrary RM/Getty Images; 33 (A), U.S. Navy/Mass Communication Specialist 2nd Class Kilho Park; 33 (B), U.S. Navy/Mass Communication Specialist 1st Class Joshua Davies; 33 (C), U.S. Navy/Petty Officer 2nd Class Ernesto Hernandez Fonte; 33 (D), blue jean images/Getty Images; 33 (E), Janice Richard/E+/Getty Images; 33 (F), Gary John Norman/The Image Bank/Getty Images; 33 (G), John Howard/Getty Images; 33 (H), Cultura RM/Zak Kendal/Getty Images; 33 (I), U.S. Air Force/Staff Sgt. Shane A. Cuomo; 33 (J), Donald Iain Smith/Blend Images RM/Getty Images; 33 (K), Terry Vine/Blend Images RM/Getty Images; 33 (L), U.S. Air Force/Staff Sgt. Renae Saylock; 33 (M), U.S. Air National Guard/Master Sgt. Mark C. Olsen; 33 (N, O), U.S. Air Force/Tech. Sgt. Samuel King Jr.; 33 (P), Cyndi Monaghan/Moment Open/Getty Images; 33 (Q), U.S. Marine Corps/Lance Cpl. Christopher Mendoza; 33 (R), U.S. Army/Timothy L. Hale, Public Affairs Specialist; 33 (S), Kendra Helmer/USAID; 33 (T), The Asahi Shimbun/Getty Images; 33 (U), U.S. Coast Guard/Petty Officer 3rd Class Dustin R. Williams; 33 (V), National Guard/Fred W. Baker III; 33 (W), U.S. Marine Corps/Lance Cpl. Glen Santy; 33 (X), Holly Powers; 33 (Y), U.S. Coast Guard/Fireman Mark Krebs; 33 (Z), Neil Brandvold/USAID; 33 (AA), U.S. Marine Corps photo/Sgt. Alfred V. Lopez; 33 (BB), BrittanyMorganPhoto.com/Courtesy MilitaryChild.org; 33 (CC), Luke Sharrett/Getty Images; 34, U.S. Air Force/Tech. Sgt. Samuel King Jr.; 35 (LE), Cyndi Monaghan/Moment Open/Getty Images; 35 (RT), Public Domain; 36 (LE), U.S. Marine Corps photo/Lance Cpl. Christopher Mendoza; 36 (CTR), U.S. Army/Timothy L. Hale, Public Affairs Specialist; 36 (RT), Kendra Helmer/USAID; 37 (LE), The Asahi Shimbun/Getty Images; 37 (CTR), U.S. Coast Guard/Petty Officer 3rd Class Dustin R. Williams; 37 (RT), National Guard/Fred W. Baker III; 38 (LE), U.S. Marine Corps/Lance Cpl. Glen Santy; 38 (RT), Holly Powers; 39 (LE), U.S. Coast Guard/Fireman Mark Krebs; 39 (RT), Neil Brandvold/USAID; 40, U.S. Marine Corps/Sgt. Alfred V. Lopez; 41, BrittanyMorganPhoto.com/Courtesy MilitaryChild.org

BRAVE
Like Me

Barbara Kerley

BRAVE
Like Me

Barbara Kerley

NATIONAL
GEOGRAPHIC

WASHINGTON, D.C.

When someone is serving their country,

far from home, they have to be brave.

Their families have to be brave.

Even their kids have to be brave.

Like me.

We spend lots of time **together ...**

until the day we have to say goodbye.

Dad gives me a huge **kiss.**

Mom wraps me up in a **hug** big enough

to last the whole time she's away.

And then they're gone.

The house is too empty.

Who is going to take **care** of me?

I look at the map, but Mom feels **far away.**

And when I'm getting ready for bed, she's just waking up.

Sometimes I feel angry Dad can't come to my game

or **sad** when he misses my show at school.

Sometimes I'm scared Mom will get hurt.

But I know she's really **careful.**

I know Dad has worked hard

to learn how to stay **safe.**

I can **talk** to Dad on the phone and on the computer.

Even when he sounds tired,

he's never too tired to hear about my day!

I can **send** letters and photos

and the pictures I draw myself.

I miss Dad every day.

But I know he's doing his job, the best he can.

And I'm doing my job the best that I can, too—

going to school, doing my homework,

and helping around the house, so that he will be

as **proud of me** as I am of him.

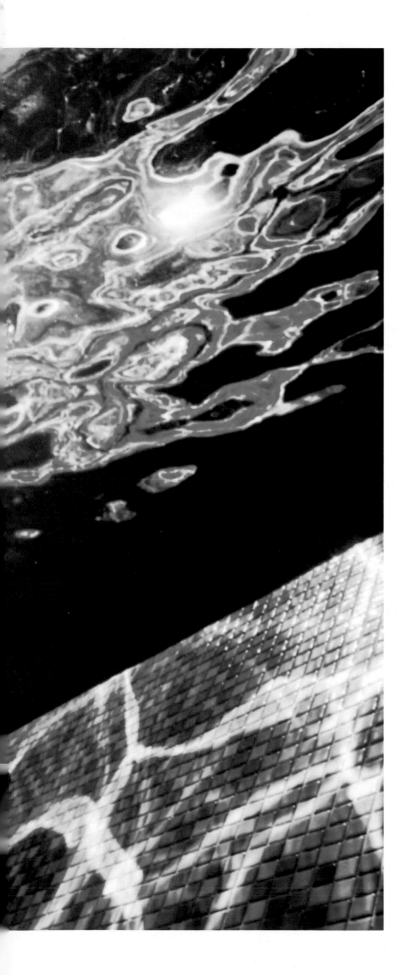

While Mom's gone, the rest of

my family helps make dinner

and reads me books

and tucks me in at night.

My neighbors and friends

take me to the park,

and the movies, and the pool.

The people who care

about me will

take care of me.

When someone is serving their country,

far from home, they think about their family all the time.

They want us to be **happy.**

Like me.

I am busy every day—with my **friends** at the park …

... with my **pets,** and even when I'm all alone.

So I'll have lots of things to talk about

and a million hugs and kisses to **share ...**

... when they come **home.**

Bravery Around the **World**

Arctic Ocean

GERMANY

UNITED
KINGDOM

U.S.

NORTH
AMERICA

ENGLAND

AFGHANISTAN

Hill Air Force Base,
Utah

Richmond,
Virginia

London

UNITED
STATES

Fort McCoy,
Wisconsin

Parlin, New Jersey

Spangdahlem
Air Base

Beijing

Northridge,
Los Angeles,
California

Little Rock
Air Force Base,
Arkansas

SPAIN

IRAQ

CHINA

Pacific
Ocean

Marine Corps Base
Camp Pendleton,
California

FLORIDA

Naval Station
Rota

San Diego,
California

Havana

Duke Field,
Eglin Air Force Base,
Florida

Tallil Air Base

Holloman
Air Force Base,
New Mexico

Fort
Hood,
Texas

CUBA

Desdunes

AFRICA

Helmand
Province

Houston,
Texas

HAITI

Port-au-Prince

Arabian
Sea

Galveston,
Texas

Disco Hill,
Margibi County

Indian
Ocean

Pacific
Ocean

LIBERIA

Atlantic
Ocean

SOUTH
AMERICA

AUSTRALIA

MAP KEY

Country where
photo originated

SOUTH
AFRICA

Pretoria

MANAWATU-
WANGANUI

NEW
ZEALAND

Location of photo

0   2000 MILES

0   2000 KILOMETERS

Hanging on to Dad
at Spangdahlem Air Base, **Germany**

Flying high
at Camp Pendleton,
California, U.S.A.

Side by side aboard the
U.S.S. *Bonhomme Richard*
in **San Diego, California, U.S.A.**

Coming in for a landing
at Little Rock Air Force Base,
Arkansas, U.S.A.

Family fun
at the neighborhood park, **U.S.A.**

A big kiss at
Holloman Air Force Base,
New Mexico, U.S.A.

A warm hug
in **Richmond, Virginia, U.S.A.**

Waiting and wondering
in **London, England**

Making sense of the map
at home

Missing the ball—and Dad—
on the soccer field

Suiting up aboard the
U.S.S. *Harry S. Truman*
in the **Arabian Sea**

Keeping in touch aboard
the U.S.N.S. *Spearhead*
in the **Atlantic Ocean**

Staying safe
in **Helmand Province, Afghanistan**

A little screen time
in **Beijing, China**

Saying "hi" to Mom
with big pink hearts

Washing up
in **Florida, U.S.A.**

Hitting the books
after school

Getting wet
in **England**

Writing home
from Tallil Air Base, **Iraq**

Playing with pals
in **Manawatu, New Zealand**

A fuzzy snuggle
in **Houston, Texas, U.S.A.**

Awaiting arrival
at Hill Air Force Base, **Utah, U.S.A.**

A sweet surprise
in **Parlin, New Jersey, U.S.A.**

All smiles
at Eglin Air Force Base,
Florida, U.S.A.

A happy hug
at Eglin Air Force Base,
Florida, U.S.A.

A letter to Mom
on a colorful page

Climbing the ropes
at Naval Station Rota, **Spain**

Plotting a course
at Fort McCoy, **Wisconsin, U.S.A.**

Rebuilding lives
in **Port-au-Prince, Haiti**

Diplomacy at work
in **Havana, Cuba**

Helicopter training
off **Galveston, Texas, U.S.A.**

A veterinary clinic
in **Desdunes, Haiti**

Sharing a feast
in **Helmand Province, Afghanistan**

Helping school kids
in **Pretoria, South Africa**

Patrolling the waters
in the **Atlantic Ocean**

Bringing medical care
to **Disco Hill, Margibi County,
Liberia**

Racing for a win
at Camp Pendleton,
California, U.S.A.

Polka dots and smiles
at Fort Hood,
Texas, U.S.A.

The best part of coming home
to **Northridge, California, U.S.A.**

Dealing With Separation

When you talk to families about what it's like to have Mom or Dad serving overseas, they'll tell you it's hard—for everyone. Sometimes kids feel sad or scared. They miss their mom or dad and worry about them. Moms and dads overseas miss everyday things like family dinners and watching a movie together. They wish they could be home for special occasions like birthdays and holidays.

One thing that helps is to stay connected with Mom or Dad through emails and phone calls, and especially seeing and hearing them during video chats on the computer.

It also really helps to stay busy and have fun! Playing sports or having a favorite hobby makes it easier to pass the time while Mom or Dad is gone. Spending time with friends and cuddling with pets help, too.

And many families like to plan all the fun things they will do when Mom or Dad comes home and the whole family can spend lots of time—together.

. . . .

"Enjoy every day,
even if the circumstances
are **less than perfect.**"

—Megan

Being **Brave** Means...

"Listening to the **little voice inside you,** no matter what anyone else tells you, **and acting on it.**"

—Erin

"**Doing something** you really don't **want** to do, when you don't **have** to do it, and when no one will know if you don't do it."

—Jack

"**Not afraid** to do something and always being **strong** no matter what."

—Elisia

"Brave means someone who **sacrifices everything** to do good, to help others. To be there when someone isn't and to be that **helping hand** in any crisis."

—Kristina

"Brave means that **you can do anything!**"

—Claire

Who **Serves?**

Many of the men and women who serve the United States work for the U.S. Armed Forces in more than 100 countries around the world. The U.S. Armed Forces has five branches: the Army, the Marine Corps, the Navy, the Air Force, and the Coast Guard.

The main goal of the Armed Forces is to prevent war and keep our country safe. When combat is necessary, members of the Armed Forces conduct missions on land, on sea, in the air, and even in cyberspace.

More often, however, servicemen and servicewomen work to maintain security. They protect military bases, embassies, and airports. They bring stability to areas of conflict. They prevent piracy and the transport of illegal drugs.

The U.S. Armed Forces also brings humanitarian aid to people all over the world. Servicemen and servicewomen build schools and hospitals, train health care workers, and transport medical supplies and books. Doctors and dentists provide medical care. Even veterinarians travel to other countries to treat livestock.

After a natural disaster like an earthquake, hurricane, or landslide, the military sends medical personnel to treat the injured. They deliver emergency supplies of food, water, and blankets. They establish communication systems to help relief agencies begin recovery work.

These humanitarian efforts strengthen the United States' relationships with other countries and help bring peace and stability to other parts of the world.

The members of the U.S. Armed Forces also have responsibilities that go beyond combat and humanitarian assistance. Their services play a major role in noncombat areas such as the

Department of Health and Human Services and the Department of Commerce. Military members also have opportunities for rotational assignments with other federal and nonfederal agencies.

Civilians also serve the United States far from home. Because our world is so interconnected, many of our government agencies have representatives overseas to help protect Americans from crime and ensure our prosperity. Many of these men and women work for the Department of State, Agency for International Development (USAID), Peace Corps, Federal Bureau of Investigation (FBI), Central Intelligence Agency (CIA), Drug Enforcement Administration (DEA), Department of Agriculture (USDA), Department of Commerce, and Centers for Disease Control and Prevention (CDC). Also, there are many private contractors working for these various groups abroad.

Employees of the Department of State work in U.S. embassies and consulates to increase our understanding of the politics and economics of other countries around the world. State Department workers support U.S. citizens living or traveling abroad. They also engage in diplomacy—explaining U.S. policy and thought to others to promote understanding and encourage peaceful and collaborative relationships among cultures.

USAID, which is also part of the Department of State, helps promote the United States' interests abroad by helping bring prosperity to developing countries. In hundreds of projects around the world, USAID employees work to fight poverty and food insecurity. They bring clean water to communities and help protect the environment. They enhance educational opportunities. They promote political stability and the spread of democracy.

Many other government agencies send men and women to work overseas. Peace Corps volunteers serve in local communities worldwide to address such issues as food security, disease prevention, and gender equality. The FBI fights criminal and terrorist threats to our national security. The CIA gathers information on political and economic developments in other countries. The DEA works to stop the manufacture and trafficking of illegal drugs. The USDA supports global food production, safety, access, and trade. The Department of Commerce promotes economic growth and sustainability. The CDC protects the nation's health and security.

Of course, there are also civilians working for the Department of Defense (DoD) in the departments of the Army, Navy, and Air Force alongside the servicemen and servicewomen at home and abroad.

A Note to **Caregivers**

As the images on these pages so beautifully illustrate, the military child looks just like any other child. What distinguishes them are the unique experiences they have that are particularly related to their parents' or caretakers' military service. Whether those experiences include moving (most military kids move six to nine times in their K–12 education years), coping with separation from their parent, or worrying about their parent's safety, military children deal frequently with transition. How children cope with the challenges related to a military lifestyle depends on the individual child and family, but there are many things adults can do to provide a supportive environment.

• • • • • • • • • • • • •

"The kids are far **braver** than I am in their ability to endure the separation and stay **positive.**" —Rich

We believe parents and other caretakers are a child's first and most important advocates. An engaged parent recognizes needs and behaviors in their child well before others do and can seek appropriate help if necessary. Becoming an engaged or informed caregiver isn't difficult. It can be as simple as reading to your child on a regular basis, actively listening to them as they talk about their day, or seeking updates from their teacher or other adults in their lives. It's especially important to be aware of any differences in behavior or attitudes during periods of change that might accompany a move or a parent's assignment away from home. Some suggestions to ensure that conditions at home reflect a positive learning environment are:

- **Establish a daily family routine.** Provide time and a quiet place to study, assign responsibility for household chores, and be firm about bedtime and having dinner together.

"Try to **stay busy,** always **talk to someone** when you feel bad." —Devon

• • • • • • • • • • • • •

- **Monitor out-of-school activities.** Set limits on TV-watching, check up on children when parents are not home, and arrange after-school activities and supervised care.

- **Model the value of learning, self-discipline, and hard work.** Communicate through questions and conversation, and demonstrate that achievement comes from working hard.

- **Express high but realistic expectations for achievement.** Set goals and standards appropriate for a child's age and maturity level, recognize and encourage special talents, and share successes with friends and family.

- **Encourage children's development and progress in school.** Maintain a warm and supportive home, show interest in children's progress at school, help with homework, discuss the value of a good education and possible career options, and stay in touch with teachers and school staff.

- **Encourage reading, writing, and discussions among family members.** Read and listen to children read; talk about what is being read.

 At the Military Child Education Coalition® (MCEC), our work informs the caring adults in the lives of military and veteran-connected children. Programs and services are designed to develop skills and strategies to help young people thrive through life's events. For a wealth of information and helpful tips to ensure a great education for your child, please visit www.MilitaryChild.org.

• • • • • • • • • • • • •

"Be **happy** that your parents are **helping others."** —Andres

Further **Resources**

4-H Military Partnerships
4-hmilitarypartnerships.org

Boys & Girls Clubs of America
bgca.org/military/Pages/default.aspx
Provides programs for military families

Department of Defense's National Center for Telehealth & Technology
Military Kids Connect
militarykidsconnect.dcoe.mil

***The Future of Children* Journal**
militarychild.org/the-future-of-children-journal
Provides a wealth of information about
military kids

Military Child Education Coalition
schoolquest.org
homeroom.militarychild.org
Provides support to parents, teachers,
and health professionals

PBS
pbs.org/parents/cominghome/activities.html

Sesame Street
Talk, Listen, Connect Toolkit
sesamestreet.org/parents/topicsandactivities/
toolkits/tlc
"Sesame Street for Military Families"
An iTunes app that provides a variety of resources

YMCA Military Outreach
ymca.net/military-outreach
Provides membership and respite child care

· · · · · · · · · · · · · ·

"When everyone's daddy
is wearing the **same
uniform** and you haven't
seen your daddy
for a while, you can
sometimes **accidentally
hug the wrong guy.**
That's embarrassing!"—Mia

"I like to have **something small** I carry on me **from each of them.** When I come home, I usually bring a small rock for each of them from **the places I go."** —John

"I took one of their **favorite teddy bears,** and I took **photos** of Teddy all throughout my deployment." —Kerry